End of Season

An anthology of award-winning poetry

from the inaugural
Tom Howard Poetry Contest

The Tom Howard Poetry Contest

A premier Literary Competition for Original Creative Writing in Poetry or Verse in any Style and on any Theme

US$5,350 in Cash Prizes, plus Publication (if desired) in an Anthology of Winning Entries

Closing date: September 30, each year

Entries may be submitted online at http://www.winningwriters.com

Entry forms are not required for this Contest.

Entry fees are $7 for every 25 lines (or part thereof).

There is no maximum limit on the number of lines (or number of entries) you may submit.

ALL TYPES AND GENRES OF POETRY ARE ACCEPTED

END OF SEASON

AN ANTHOLOGY OF AWARD-WINNING POETRY

from the inaugural
Tom Howard Poetry Contest
(plus six bonus poems by the editor)

edited by

John Howard Reid

Published by Lulu Books
If it's a good book, it's a Lulu!

Please apply to
johnreid@mail.qango.com

FIRST PRINTING: DECEMBER 2003

NEW EDITION: MARCH 2004

REVISED EDITION: JULY 2004

NEW EDITION: JANUARY 2009

Lulu Books
http://www.lulu.com/filmindex

ISBN: 978-0-557-02289-2

CONTENTS

1. **Jennie Herrera**: "Fritillary" {First Prize}

2. **Adam Wallace**: "Jeremy Johnson Jackson the Third" {Third Prize}

3. **Adam Wallace**: "Bike Riding" {Most Highly Commended}

4. **Pali Munasinghe**: "No More Wars" {Highly Commended}

5. **Trudy Davis**: "An Alien in Cyberspace" {Short-listed}

6. **Jean MacDonald**: "Over the Road, Down by the Creek" {Most Highly Commended}

7. **Evelyn Wright**: "Ode to Politicians" {Commended}

8. **Rochelle Manners**: "Look at you" {Commended.}

9. **Eve Ryfkah**: "Eclipse" {Short-listed}

10. **Nana Ollerenshaw**: "Mackay" {Most Highly Commended}

11. **Jade Walker**: "War" {Short-listed}

12. **Jacqueline Cooke**: "End of Season" {Most Highly Commended}

13. **Jonathan Elsom**: "Dawn at the Cross" {Most Highly Commended}

14. **Susan Kruss**: "Midway" {Short-listed}

15. **Michael P. Mardel**: "South west down-under" {Very Highly Commended}

16. **Rachel J. Johnson**: "Words Elude Me" {Short-listed}

17. **Michael Jones**: "My Palm Beach Girl" {Short-listed}

18. **John Irvine**: "Dust Storm" {Most Highly Commended}

19. **Allistair R. Clarke**: "Colac" {Commended}

20. **David O'Connell**: "following" {Most Highly Commended}

21. **Yvonne Schneider**: "Forever Young" {Commended}

22. **Agnes Craig**: "Something in Common" {Commended}

23. **Gavin S. Austin**: "In the Garden" {Most Highly Commended}

24. **Kristen R. Heyl**: "Hindsight 20/20" {Highly Commended}

25. **Su Nash**: "Nothing" {Highly Commended}

26. **Su Nash**: "White Moths" {Commended}

27. **Sook-Moy Yew**: "A Mesmerizing World" {Commended}

28. **Lahta Stephens**: "Tiny Island" {Short-listed}

29. **Kylie Hooklyn**: "Shy" {Short-listed}

30. **Aaron Goldsmith**: "Lenni and I" {Commended}

31. **Fiona Sievers**: "when his father died" {Commended}

32. **Pamela Blackburn**: "A First Kiss" {Most Highly Commended}

33. **Suzanne Edgar**: "The Ring-Maker" {Highly Commended}

34. **Suzanne Edgar**: "Night-Shift" {Highly Commended}

35. **Ann Tregenza**: "Train Journey" {Second Prize}

36. **John H. Reid**: "Escape to Paradise"

37. **John H. Reid**: "The Actor Deprived of His Voice"

38. **J. Reid**: "Art Gallery to Circular Quay"

39. **John Howard Reid & Dee C. Konrad**: "A Lion's Lion"

40. **John Howard Reid**: "Access Denied"

41. **John Howard Reid**: "Malalam"

42. **John Howard Reid**: "Magic"

Special Addendum: Some Guidelines for entering the Tom Howard Poetry Contest

FRITILLARY

by **Jennie Herrera**

Sweet bright grasses fringed about a secret cove,
With little rasping voices, softer than the waves that
curl,
Softer than the winds that trill a harmony across the
dunes,
    Telling tales …
Butterflies brown and white, with lead-light marks
upon their wings
With tiny cooing voices, softer than terns, softer far
than dolphin gulls,
Softer than a million sand midges with their tiny
beating wings,
    Telling tales …
'We saw it there', 'it was so long ago', 'they passed
the story on'
'Years and countless years', 'a hundred generations, *I*
dare suggest'
'It flew, our ancestors claimed, like a thing
possessed'
    Telling tales …
'How it cried!'—'like a beast bled, *I* heard, 'and all
the while
A flapping', 'A noise *my* family passed to me, like a
clap of thunder'
—'In a summer storm'—They drowsed together, in
lush seed-head,
    Telling tales …

Victualling: Mr. Philobert Jenkins' Account

That picher, sir? A fine ship she were, on the
Nitrate run a while—carried forty men—and
Shorty Sloane—
I've been with the firm near forty years, seen
the fam'ly
Come and go—but it's the ships you
remember—Yes, sir?
Biscuits?—Mr. Mullins will serve you, sir—It
were port
Not brandy for Lord 'amer's yacht—Beg
yours—
Shorty Sloane? I remember 'im particular—
Brought bad luck,
The men said, casual-like—Couldn't see it
meself—but never sailed.
No sir—Salt, sir? Nine and sixpence, that'll
be—
They paid 'im orf, Shorty, left 'im in this port
and that—
Poor Shorty—couldn't leave the sea alone—
'e finally got a berth in 'obart Town—'e
loved that ship,
And Shorty weren't a sentimental man—a
perfect clipper—
Pine—'aven't seen the 'uon pine, sir? Lovely,
yellow wood.
Made fine ships, that it did … Loved 'er like a
son, they said.
Went overboard one night, left a note—
To give the ship good luck, 'e wrote, poor
bloke—
Quaffed the cap'n's best French brandy, 'fore
'e done the deed,
No rum for Shorty Sloane when 'e set out for
'eaven, like—

And you know what, sir? Didn't do no good
… that fine clipper,
Strong as they make 'em, plied the sea with
perfect pitch, regal like,
Should've seen 'er, sir—and ran before the
wind, straight
Into an open shore—some said it were the
skipper at that
Fine French brandy—but that weren't no
comfort to poor Shorty—
… Now your rope, sir, 'awser-laid … 'emp,
sir, sisal or coir?

'The way it fell, like a stricken beast', 'great gushing
gouts, they said'
'Not a story for the young'—'And cries', 'More a
bellow, in *my* version'
'A wounded roar, *I* heard … like a dragon stabbed'—
'And then the stalks broke'
 Telling tales …
'It had a name, they saw, in gilt upon its head';—
'S.S. Fri— l ' 'It wore away
With time, a shadow of a name'; the fritillaries gather
round these wormholes
In the weathered wood; a faint sweet fragrance still
there about the worn-our ribs,
 Telling tales …

JEREMY JOHNSON JACKSON THE THIRD

by **Adam Wallace**

I love my teddy bear.
I call him Jeremy Johnson Jackson the Third.
Jez for short.
Jeremy Johnson Jackson the Third.
I love my teddy bear.
He always gets close when I need him.
He's so soft, he's so cuddly.
Sometimes my tears just disappear into his fur.
I love my teddy bear.
I talk to him, even though he can't talk back.
Sometimes we have tea, oh la dee da, how nice.
He's such a good listener.
I love my teddy bear.
He's getting old now.
He's falling apart, a bit more with every squeeze.
I don't want him to go.
I love my teddy bear.
I don't care that I can get another, new teddy bear.
I want my Jeremy Johnson Jackson the Third!
I never want another teddy bear!!!!
I love my teddy bear.
The last night. Mum says he has to be thrown out
tomorrow.
We talk, as usual, and I hold him closer than ever.
My tears stain his fur.
I'll always love my teddy bear.

BIKE RIDING

by **Adam Wallace**

I go real fast on my bike.
John doesn't.
He's my best friend, but boy does he ride slow.
When I ride real fast, my eyes get water in 'em.
John rides slow.
His eyes don't get water.
I ride through puddles real fast.
John doesn't.
He goes round 'em.
My Mum yells at me 'cos there's mud dots on my t-
shirt.
John's mum doesn't yell.
John doesn't have dots.
If John rode through puddles, no water would spray
up.
Too slow, John!
I go over dirt jumps real fast, and fly through the air.
Mud dots, eyes watering, wind in my face, the works.
John goes over jumps slow and safe.
He doesn't even get in the air.
It's not a jump for John, it's a bump.
Sometimes, because I go pretty hard, I might lose
control.
Mum has to put band-aids and cream on where I
stacked and cut myself.
John doesn't stack.
If he did, he wouldn't cut himself 'cos he'd be going
too slow.
I'd rather get cuts and get yelled at and get mud dots
and stuff.
You know what I mean.

NO MORE WARS

by **Pali Munasinghe**

Only now I hear,
The song of the brook,
Dancing through the woods,
Like a silver snake.
I sit on my chair,
With a wooden slab for a seat,
A dethroned queen, re-throned.

Looming ahead like a misfortune,
Darkness swallowed us.
Creeping under thorn bushes,
We hid hardly daring to breathe.
They are full of ripe berries now,
Sweet and sour how lovely!.
Of course, I had not tasted them in years.

Moist moving images,
Of children, laughing, chattering,
Are clear now, seen through a shiny mirror.
Constriction in the throat, cheek in the hand,
Are all of the past

A burden pressing me down,
Has been lifted,
Birds, come and sing,
I'll dance to the tune.

AN ALIEN IN CYBERSPACE

by **Trudy Davis**

I was born too long ago.

My home was safe and stable.
My parents' words laid down the law
Of everything there was to know;
I did what I was able.

    then Chaos came –
    Progress was its name –
    relentlessly making its way…

the floodgates opened –
surfing became
essential to survive

    newborn babes learnt
    how to ride
    the ever-shifting tide

my faint efforts
to stay afloat
did not succeed for long

my stable home
wrecked by the flood
protects me no more

I am an Alien –
surrounded by invaders
who speak a foreign tongue

I *was* born too long ago

OVER THE ROAD, DOWN BY THE CREEK

by **Jean MacDonald**

There were horses, once, over the road.

Knee deep in mist and grass they'd stand

On Autumn mornings, down by the creek.

Old pine trees cluttered the paddock;

On their bare top branches cockatoos gathered

To shout their rage in the Summer twilight

Wheeling and shrieking, but always coming back.

In Winter the green would stand frost-stiff

Stark against the wire fence;

Silence broken by racketing crows

Strung loose on a telegraph wire.

It's all gone now.

The trees wrenched from the ground

The horses carried, protesting, away

And the long green stamped and churned in the mud.

The land stands clearly divided

Neat squares for neat suburban homes

Soon only the ghosts of horses will float in the morning mist

Down by the creek.

ODE TO POLITICIANS

by **Evelyn Wright**

Why speak empty words
to echo in our puzzled afterthoughts?
Are they said to still the voices
you do not wish to hear,
or to ease a nagging conscience
temporarily?
Can't your closed, uncaring minds
sense the disappointment
as hope slowly dwindles
and bitter cynicism takes its place?
Those slick and sugary words
spoken with such false sincerity
mean no more than the wind
sighing through the trees —

yet they leave such devastation in their
wake;
soft showers that turn
into destructive gales,
destroying future trust.

These are your promises!

LOOK AT YOU

by **Rochelle Manners**

But when I look at you

I see a part of me

Passing through

I see all my love

    . . . .slip away

ECLIPSE

by **Eve Ryfkah**

but that's another story
book tale of the cow
jumps over moo-light
sonata playing through
open farmhouse door

We lie on clover
pungent white flower
everywhere
You hold a dandelion
I want to stroke its feathers
into the soft west wind
The sun slips away amethyst

The cow dozes in the barn

Jacaranda purples front yard
covers our hair like a crown
You touch me a prayer
returned in murmur
Your caresses tease
dilatory like a lime caterpillar
slipping across my heart
We croon under blue moon

Darkened stars envy our total eclipse

MACKAY

by **Nana Ollerenshaw**

The yellow town blazes by a green sea.
The tide eats footprints on the sand
like a cat prowling.

The old and the new lie uneasily together.
Tuscan high rise prick the flatness
of a coastal plain and sea
where boats marina bright like seagulls rest

and homes with iron hats sit stolid in the heat
latticed with neglect. Their stilts provide
a cellar from the sun, and storage
for the junk of living.

Verandahs tell of time and cups of tea,
laundry, corner stores, the heat.
People stay put, make ends meet,
palms clack with fronds like ladders
as the day sleeps.

WAR

(cinquain)

by **Jade Walker**

I wait.
Hours linger.
There is no news.
Will he come back to me alive?
I hope.

END OF SEASON

by **Jacqueline Cooke**

I still catch my breath when I remember how

his footprints left no trace on the wet, rippled beach.

He hesitated — that's when I knew he was hoping it

wouldn't be me.

I reached to feel his warm skin, licked the salt off my

fingers.

He turned from my anxious, trembling touch.

All I heard was the sharp stillness of the dune drift

grass,

and a dog barking at the far end, near the cliff.

I was afraid to speak

seeing in his blank stare nothing

but the heavy heat speckling the sand,

each grain intense with indifferent lies.

A dinghy engine spluttered and died.

Someone looked through the green blinds in the
white house.

Two people laughed as they walked by.

He moved away, masking his deceit, threw a pebble
into the water,

his suntanned curves and secret thirsty hollows

already greedy for the next summer and the next too

eager girl.

DAWN AT THE CROSS

by **Jonathan Elsom**

Like spritely aproned waiters

Ibis stalk,

And through bare autumn leaves

Eddying to catch crisp daybreak gusts

The fountain glisters

Like a silvered dandelion,

Showering its icelets

'Gainst the new formed day.

Macleay Street sheds its frowsty

Morning light,

Stark plane trees march towards The Bay,

And further up The Cross

Street sweepers edge

The night's detritus from dishevelled streets,

While huddled sleepers

Mouth unrealised dreams

In shopfront doors against the cold,

And distant sirens

Howling to the wind

Announce the dawning of another day.

MIDWAY

by **Susan Kruss**

I wake to the sound of wood pigeons
clock-clocking under the apple tree
sated in a wave of windfalls.

Cider breeze stirs the lace curtains
leaving a fine mist of gold particles
and the scent of split wood.

Behind the laden branches
a brown hill grows;
damp colours of honey
dry to a consistency of biscuit.

Two front-end loaders spin around on
top
backwards and forwards – tonka toys
in a sandpit scraping wide swathes.

Lit at night by strings of orange globes
two white spotlights like giant
magnets –
moths drift to their deaths.

All day the hopper sucks in trees
and spits out chips. All night
the loader pours the hill
into the hold of a black ship.

By morning the hill
has become a mound
the hopper is at full speed.

The ship slides out of the quay
wrapped in a white blanket
sounding its horn through bay fog.

In the rail yard a new row
of open trucks piled high with logs
and at the security gate
another semi-trailer arrives with a full
load.

SOUTH WEST
down-under

by **Michael P. Mardel**

We were soaked
Soaking
Soaking up the land
Soaking up the miles
The kilometres
Daily traversing
Only resting at night
Driven relentlessly onwards
Infrequent stops
Soaking up the landscape
Soaked by the showers
Vision soaked by
Rain-splattered windows
Salt-sticky panes
Eventually washed
By the soaking showers
Green grasses soaked
Trees and leaves dripping
Our souls soaked
Drawn down
Into the land
The land down-under

WORDS ELUDE ME

by **Rachel J. Johnson**

Words elude me.
I see the shapes of words
inside.
What are the images?
Where can my thoughts burst through,
enabling speech to equal me?
When will the shapes of my words
find the place to become?
Words are
pounding my subconscious thought,
skipping as a stone across the river.
I stutter
always
to catch up.

MY PALM BEACH GIRL

by **Michael Jones**

Now, when I think of her,
I think of dappled shadows,
beneath the trees
and sunlight glittering on a dark, blue sea.
I remember the smell of hot bread, in the morning,
and martinis at lunch, on the beach,
Under the pink umbrella —
that umbrella bright as hope against the sky,
against the hibiscus and the geranium,
and laughter in the air,
as if the world and all its pleasures
would last forever —
as if we would be young and beautiful,
For each other
Always.

I think of picnics in the countryside,
as we drove across France
in September,
in the fading summer heat,
the car hood down and
the wind in our bleached hair,
still stiff from the salt
of some small Mediterranean beach,
now left behind along the way,
disappearing into the past
as we sped north

between the rows of poplars.

There's a baguette and some brie, some cold ham,
on the back seat,
with a basket of late strawberries
and the local wine in plastic cups,
and the autumn heat on our necks
as we made love in the grass of some neglected field,
in Provence or the Langue d'Oc, or in the Var.

Or, sometimes, perhaps,
an omelette and green salad on the terrace
of some small hotel - the Lion d'Or?
hanging over the river,
with the grey stone houses of the village
clinging to the rocks across the slow
and rippling water.

These are the things that I recall
of all those years we were in love,
when it seemed that time
did not pass at all,
that we would never grow old
nor die.

And now, as I recall those days,
I ask myself,
Where have those years all gone,
and you?
And all the joy?

DUST STORM

by **John Irvine**

Darkness presses down
with a terrible and inexorable force.
Sunlight, only a heartbeat ago
golden and friendly

is now blood red and ominous,
as sand, billowing a kilometre high,
snuffs out reality.

The air is thick and dry—yet almost viscous.
Breathing is obscenely loud and laboured
in the pre-storm quiet.

There is no other sound.

Insects, and even the boisterous cockatoos
have shut down their cacophony.
Kangaroos squat, sheltering
beneath gnarled mallee trees.

Any voice, imprudently loud,
is swallowed instantly
by the grasping, enveloping
miasma of airborne soil.

Doors are shut and bolted,
screens secured, animals indoors.
Cats and dogs cowering,
utterly soundless. Shivering.

Just another summer dust storm,
carrying away in its unsympathetic arms
our livelihood. Our future. Our home.

Again.

Still, as we all sit around
the long slab of rough wood
we call our kitchen table,
holding hands against
the whispering holocaust
that is approaching,

we know that with the passing of time
our sun will return,
golden again, with a clear face,

and the memory of this will be recorded as
just another chapter of daily life in the outback.
The cycle of seasons passes,
and we endure.

We endure.

COLAC

by **Allistair R. Clarke**

Inchoate thoughts self-reflected

A peremptory instruction; a rushed taxi trip for the
5:10 pm Warrnambool train

Merging, then disentangling from the 'John Brack,
Collins St, 5 pm' crowd

Into a Drysdalesque Spencer Street terminus -
Melbourne, 1955

Trip beginning. Geelong, Moriac, Winchelsea: the
closer to Colac, the more attenuated the city's
influence

7:32 pm, Colac. The city no longer exists. Just
Colac now

A light rain falls, defining cones of light from station
lampposts

Into Lennie Watts' taxi...Local

gossip...Grandparents'...Welcoming!

Down the hall, past a reproduction of Turner's
'Fighting Temeraire'

The Dining Room - Scottish memorabilia: a plaque
of Robbie Burns; the McKenzie tartan and motto
'Luceo Non Uro' (I shine but don't burn)

A week or more of this. Languorous days punctuated
by sensory perceptions: casseroles cooking; baker
back-door conversing; Evening Star splitting the
twilight blue veil

COLAC - time's depredations have not lessened its
visceral epiphany

following

by **David O'Connell**

the small dog, the persistent drag
of its injured shuffle - I followed it
through the streets, a casual
pursuit between market stalls, a meeting
of aged men close to death and not
caring, women seated at tables
wiping their mouths
in a reflex, bench-pressing youths
charging their egos,
girls with lollipops stuck
to their hips, table-erecters generating
steam from their mouths to double
my vision, but I never
lost sight of the dog, melting
around corners, from landmark
to landfill, strangers unconsciously
stepping out of its way, never pausing
to smell the scraps on the road. I saw
chunks dissolve from its coat, an ear
losing contour and part of its tail, getting
no closer, falling
no further behind, a willing participant -
this could have ended at any
moment, tempting me as it did, far
from a comfort zone of sickeningly
familiar surroundings, the tiny
new dent in my car, dragged on, in awe

of that steady, shuffling stride,
before finally it staggered
through a hole of missing bricks
and the path became too narrow
to follow; I bent, gripping
my knees, as the trail of invisible
footprints faded ahead, not seeking
an alternative route.
I simply settled
for never
encountering that face
and I knew
it would come back
to haunt me.

FOREVER YOUNG

by **Yvonne Schneider**

Their lives are gone, cut short by tragedy
A wilful hand, some other country's cause
And death has come before its meant to be
Families mourn their loss; great nations pause.
We live where freedom is a way of life
We watch our children grow and reach their prime
In a land not torn by wars and strife
Some left our shores to die before their time.
They were not soldiers gone to fight the foe
We watched them leave, bound for a distant shore
To holiday, have fun, how could we know
Our sons and daughters we would see no more?
How precious are the memories we hold
Of those we love who never will grow old.

SOMETHING IN COMMON

by **Agnes Craig**

Me
and a black dog
walking together
me gathering
my thoughts
he sniffing
the ground
each of us
on the same road
each of us
searching for something
both of us
with limited freedom

hampered and
shackled by love.

IN THE GARDEN

by **Gavin S. Austin**

Christmas, the city is ringed with flames,
and the sky glows apocalyptic-orange as it rains ash.
In the garden of The Sacred Heart, beneath your window,
I sit on the seat where we once sat:
your bony hand on my thigh,
and look past the fountain toward Mary.
Her supplicant plaster palms face me
as she avoids my stare and gazes into middle-distance;
a bougainvillea vine lies bleeding at her feet.

Above me death waits at the end of each corridor,
lingers silently in the dimly lit rooms
or rattles alarmingly in pallid throats.
You told me you loved me -
that I had been a wonderful friend.
Yet I question if I did all there was to be done.
And if you saw my carefully veiled tears
as I pretended not to know what you meant
by "the dark vehicle is waiting."

First published in the e-journal *Red River Review*

HINDSIGHT 20/20

by **Kristen R. Heyl**

Ever wish you could take back
those defining moments in life
that has allowed good things
to slip through your fingers?

Ever wish you could draw
upon someone else's strengths
to overcome your weaknesses
so you could be a complete package?

Ever wish that for once
just once you couldn't
mess things up and make
life harder for yourself?

Ever wish that you could let
down your defenses and be free
from the restraints of years
of pent up hurt?

Ever wish you could just follow your heart
without your mind jumping in?

Ever wish you were someone else?

NOTHING

(Subtitled: A BIG, FAT, NOTHING)

by **Su Nash**

I like to play the Lotto

I buy it every week

I dream big dreams of winning

But even as I speak

It's always the same

It's never my name

A big, fat, nothing.

I pick numbers out at random

Or choose my favourite few

Buy quickpicks, and syndicates

What more can I do?

It's always the same

It's never my name

A big, fat, nothing.

I'd love to cruise some islands

Or buy a giant house

Dive a Porsche, *and* a Jaguar -

Wouldn't that be grouse?

It's always the same

It's never my name

A big, fat, nothing.

We've four agents in my town

Not one of them admits

I am keeping them and theirs

In a style that's really rich

And it's *still* the same

It's never my name

A big, fat, nothing.

One day I'm going to win

The big Lotto in the sky

Saint Peter at the Pearly Gates

Will look me in the eye

I know that it's a shame

There's no tick for your name

You're down below —Beelzebubbing

And I'll cry "What for me

No million dollar spending spree?

Thanks a lot Saint Peter for

A big fat NOTHING!"

WHITE MOTHS

(With apologies to Mary Oliver)

by **Su Nash**

There's a kind of white moth, I don't know

If it speaks its life to dreaming hills;

For it is on a dreaming hill

That my lover and I lie slow

While white moths fly and dip and frill

Or rest unclear

On grassy spear.

And in the dying day,

Enshrouded in love's prize,

Does my fragile heart beat

In the shadow of white lies?

I don't know.

A MESMERIZING WORLD

by **Sook-Moy Yew**

Glittering peacocks strut with ease,

Dancing daffodils sing in the breeze,

Quivering porcupines show their might,

Fearsome rattlesnakes poise to strike,

Steely armadillos roam and roll,

Pretty periwinkles overflow,

Graceful gazelles race along,

Busy beavers chop and chomp.

Ours is a living world,

A lively mesmerizing world.

TINY ISLAND

by **Lahta Stephens**

The sea slopped and puffed jellyfish

Ropes of seaweed flung to horseshoe bay

On sea sucked pebbles stricken cuttlefish

Orphaned urchins like brutalised lycees

Oh tiny island where are your kangaroos?

Squall whips shrouds over tyre indented snakes

Gully sings, unsettling black cockatoos

The casuarinas stutter in wind's wake

The sheep's perplexed baa's lost in rain

Gum leaves, gum nuts, gum trees fall on iron roofs

Mulch, grassroots and droppings clog up the drain

Once again nature shows nothing is storm proof

But inside the little shack, we drink Milo

'Seen a storm like this before?' 'I dunno.'

SHY

by **Kylie Hooklyn**

There are four walls around me
the strong and silent type
they are my barrier from happiness
as well as fear.

Funny how I wish them gone
when secretly I employ them
then after they have served me well
I dream of their destruction.

Lenni and I

by **Aaron Goldsmith**

Selfish cat.
All you want is to sit upon my lap
and encourage my petting
with your throbbing purrs.
I always wonder if we would still be friends
if you could understand
all the abuse I throw at you
cloaked under friendly tones.
Michel's hair was similar to yours.
But hers was long and darker
and would wind its way down,
along much different terrain.
It's amusing that the stares
that you now give to me,
I once gave to her.
I had, however, much different intent.
I would sit beside her
gazing,
begging for her attention.
She must have known,
Mustn't she have?
What is this game we played?
I think of us.
Would she be the cat,
or I?

when his father died

by **Fiona Sievers**

when his father died
he too   closed up shop
like an old
abandoned warehouse

nailed tight shut
by a hundred nails
entry barred
dark and silent

he blackened his windows
took his receiver off the hook
and went below the ground
for a short while
to adjust
to a new shade
of darkness

A FIRST KISS

by **Pamela Blackburn**

I am a flying kangaroo circling with
harnessed heart. A passenger braced before
　　descending to earth
　　The smell of exhaust fumes,
　　pulse of heat waves
　　shimmering tarmac
　　a newborn birth

I am a visitor to Raffles crushing peanut shells,
the talkative taste of Singaporean gin slings
　　sharp on my tonge
　　The scent of pliant leather
　　purchased Duty Free
　　expensive, prevailing
　　skin of the young

I am a rider on space-mountain in the dark
An explorer of foreign places far from
　　the comforts of home
　　Challenging taste buns, eating odd food,
　　I learn new customs and
　　carry a dictionary of a
　　language not known

I am an orchestra warming-up amid audience

hubbub before curtain call - a gala performance
　- like Die Fliedermaus
　Lights spot the conductor as he
　strides to his podium. When
　he raises his baton
　silence captures the house

I am childhood memories of carnival nights
A chinese lantern cavalcade snaking its way
　to a firework display
　Crackle of bonfire, scent of candle wax
　- practise launch of a life boat
　onto choppy North Seas
　I am Wedding Day

THE RING-MAKER

by **Suzanne Edgar**

Through the celibate years

the ring-maker stands at his bench

chasing perfection

in silver, steel and wood,

building rings for flirts and lovers.

They bring the scent of other worlds,

break his calm with moonstone, lapis

a sliver of petrified butterfly wing.

A lathe will spin the metal

against his shaping tool

finishing rings to flatter

immaculate hands, mother-of-pearl nails.

His are ingrained with dust

that seethes above the bench;

he stoops to the task, squinting,

quiet, a tensed and focused arc.

But nerves beneath his collar-bone

pinch and complain at night;

a surgeon using knife and drill

cuts out a core of bone.

The artist takes this core

and drives a hole through bone

pure as river stone and fit for immortality,

for the fourth finger of his strong left hand.

NIGHT SHIFT

by **Suzanne Edgar**

Waiting for light,

I breathe in, and out:

there was a nightmare riding hard

its neck all flecked with sweat.

Hoof-beat and heart-beat,

racing past my severed head

face upwards in a swamp:

I knew the thud of panic,

legs that would not move.

Thought brings no relief,

dawning fears are worse for being real

deadlines leer, a quarrel unresolved.

At last a peal of magpies

rinses morning air.

The spines of books are there

and other loyal friends, a trailing scarf

the cushion on my waiting chair.

Outside, a gum's pale edge

stands firm behind the rose

blurred in a vaguer space

between low shrubs and shadow caves.

Somewhere a cistern sings —

now the blackbird can be seen

making her little darts and runs

across the wormy green.

Minute by slow minute

the grey gives way.

For light *does* come

and even, bursting

with hail fellow, well met

slap on the back

the sun!

© 2003 by Suzanne Edgar

TRAIN JOURNEY

by **Ann Tregenza**

Good-be Adelaide, Mother and Dad.
I see you trying not to cry.
Go on cry, so will I.
The train is moving earth and sky.
You've had each other for thirty years.
Be happy, plan another tour.
I'm crying, crying, crying not to
Not to not to not to not to.
Keep up the 'Rustle of Spring' Mother.
You've played it all my life on the piano.
I tried to pillow it out at night.
You play it well, try something new.
Keep up the hymns on Sunday Dad.
I'll remember your balding head at the piano:
children's songs, duets with Mother,
with Mother, with Mother, with Mother.
Now I'm on my way outback
to my husband, waiting for his wife,
like a windmill waiting for a wind.
Will I be a gentle breeze
or whirlwind whisking him this way and that.

We stop for a while at Farrell's Flat
where tense hawks clutch taut telephone wires,
telephone wires, telephone wires.
A boy waves from a school oval
then foots a ball into the dusty air.

Reminds me of the farmer's son
who came on his motor bike after Matric.
My Mother wouldn't let me go.
Now I'm free to choose it's you,
sturdy and sure with smiling brown eyes,
smiling brown eyes, smiling brown eyes.
Thin sheep scrum the shrinking shade
in the burning midday heat of summer.
Why did all the gum trees go?
No need to count the sheep, I sleep,
wake again to the same heart beat,
ranges of mouse-backed hills each side,
a breeze to keep the windmill turning,
windmill turning, windmill turning.

Whyte Yarcowie, why do we stop?
A brown grasshopper jumps into space,
a flickering flash on an unused track,
with rustle of wings climbing the air.
Wild goats rest in the ruins of stone.
Why have all the people gone?
Will we go too from drought and loss,
drought and loss, drought and loss?
Peterborough now but gone tomorrow?
Standard gauge or not will decide.
What will be our fate my love?
Yours the conservative traditional track
of husband grows wool, is lord of all.
Good wife bakes bread, obeys, serves.
Will you like my curry and rice,
Greek music and having my say,
having my say, having my say?

This is my stop. I hold my breath.
There you are on the platform waiting.
You push your thick black hair from your brow.
There is the man I couldn't refuse.
Here is the woman you dared to include.

"End of Season"

Award-Winning Poems

The End

ESCAPE TO PARADISE

by **John Howard Reid**

Walking along by the shore,

When the tide was out,

Where sand and sea-shells mingled

Whatever conjugal dust remained

Of the millennial marriage of earth and rain,

I found an old ship's lantern,

Lodged in the sand.

Breaking free, slipping through the musty tentacles

Of jailer sea, it had buoyed to the surface,

Was borne on the embroidered cloak of the tide,

and lodged in the sand.

Barnacles crawled, curled over octangular glass,

Rust stained the sheen of many-sided hands,

Yet deep within, sealed from the search of wave and
wind,

The wick, the core, the heart was sound.

That spirit lived who'd shown the way --

Though staunched and steadied -- to impossible
lands.

And now -- escaped her cataleptic grave --

She had lodged herself in the sand.

THE ACTOR DEPRIVED OF HIS VOICE

A Post-Operative Soliloquy

For Jack Hawkins

by **John Howard Reid**

"Good morning, Jack!"

But my mirror mimes empty words.

Singing swords not just blunted

Or blurred, but violently absent.

My mouth a mere mummer's show,

Now delighting in darkness

That mummifies the Bard's metres,

Whispering not the merest scent of breath,

Not even a chant of inarticulate moans.

Is this, my golden voice, reduced to dross?

My loss, the world's; my stage now confined

To pantomimist's arts. My role's the fool,

The butt, the simpleton, the bell-bedazzled jester,

The clown.

A comedown complete and yet ever so neat —

A fortuitous topple from fire-pressure heights of

fame,

Where a rebel revelled in the drooling depths of

critics' praises,

Applauded the throngs that flocked to cruel seas,

Flattered pusillanimous ghosts at the B.B.C.,

Tweaked the world from Old Drury to River Kwai,

From Israel to Innisfail.

So hard the climb, so hardened to success,

Unaware thuggish fingers of a two-faced Fate

Were slowly throttling my silvery throat to

inoperative stone —

A triumph of Life's nothingness!

What years of patronised torment lie ahead

Until diminished contracts force my buffoonish acts

To bottoms of the bills?

Numbed, heart-torn, am I painlessly re-born

One forlorn, freakish, Fawkesian guy,

A miming mummer of another's words,

Dubbed with the curling chords

Of some second-rate ham.

The above poem won 3rd Prize in the 2003 Sun City Poetry
Awards.

ART GALLERY TO QUAY

A Boy Fifteen in '53

by **John Howard Reid**

It's a long soulless walk from Art Gallery
to Circular Quay.
The paths are petite-colonnaded.
The night watchman has a key.

Why didn't I take the bus? Simple!
They were all walled in the same dismal direction:
south.
Way down south in the land of westie heaven.
I wanted north.

Winter-raining too. Not too try-some hard,
but flecking the Galleried porticoes of Cupid's
insurrection
with tearful jests.

For all their pointed attitudes,
noses thrust so intolerantly piquant south,
no empty omnibus seemed anxious

to drive or be driven away.
Engines irresponsibly idling, sieving rain
into plumes of dust.
Cheap — Christmas djinn-jolting cheap —
at tuppence ha'penny a trip.

I'd take a tram, but is Abel worth the hunt?
The long cross-city jaunt along quest-deserted floes,
torch-lit
but fearsomely spelled
in postwar de-animated neon?

I take a punt on Fate, cut across Botanic Gardens,
side-step the barricades, squeeze perilously through
Achilles' gate.

I run Medusa's icy gauntlet...
Heart and limbs still flesh intact,
breathing fast, I shelter on the coiled steps
of a marbled, serpent-sinister, cannibalistic bank.

I wait. A tram at last. *Abel!* No need to hail.
More comfortable than spent rain-wind on cold night
frolicsome faces,
though Toastrack Abel's dangling, draughty doors
are locked open —
concertinaed right open
to welcome every drift of snow.

On slatted seats as hard as the homeless gale,
on the hunt for elusive traces of leafy coins,

I find a threepence lodged in the scuff
of overcoat pocket —
enough for a ha'penny change.

"Fez!"
No bardic tones, these!
The conductor's voice grates the roar
of a Minotaur as he swings, simian-like,
across the rumbling, tightrope walking-boards.

I placate him with my coin.

It's a long circuitous walk from Art Gallery
to Circular Quay.
(At least it was in 'fifty-three).
The paths were barricaded.
Not even trams trespass free.
But Charon, Night Conductor,
now had his stygian fee.

A LION'S LION

by **John Howard Reid & Dee C. Konrad**

A Lion met a Tiger in Phoenix one day.
They sang, they danced, and then wrote a play.

Having as tempting a time as can be,
they whirled and twirled, singing, "Diddle-Dee-Dee."

But Tiger mimed, "My role is smaller than yours;
so I'll have to provide you provocative lures:

"I'll growl, I'll prowl, I'll sing 'Cat's Pajamas';
then I'll try my hand at Fernando Lamas

"and tune my teeth with the Dalai Lama,
until I mount <u>my</u> acme of drama."

Our Lion fretted and frowned and felt at a loss;
then shaking his mane—with a magnificent toss

to imply his role as the consummate boss—
he thrust himself on a throne of green moss.

*"No way will a Lion compete with his slave,
so button your bellows and learn to behave!"*

Tiger turned tail, and conceding defeat,
with an almighty wail, his retreat was complete.

Lion felt sad at his role rival's stance,
so he reined and restrained his victory dance.

No play's worth playing with only one player.
So, concocting a plot, layer by layer,

he changed Tiger's part to a Fox or a Frog.
But Tiger bounced back from his fuzzy fog

with a wail and a howl and a you-know-how,
shrieking, "Lie low, Lion, you'll pay piper now!

"A Tiger I am, a Tiger I'll be!
Just try to buckle the bold bounty of me."

Lion, unfazed, looked tight in Tiger's eyes,
as if amazed at that critter's outcries.

"Can you act like a frog, a fox or a bear?"
"Mais oui! That's as easy as eating a pear!"

*"A wombat, giraffe, armadillo or ape?
And skip skirmishes with all four on tape?"*

"No way, José! Why should I act the goat?
I'd rather be cast as a farmyard shoat!

"But nothing would give me greater pleasure,
in impromptu style, to tape your measure!

"A giraffe, Sir Lion? I'll ape you on toast
and serve you all four as a succulent roast!"

*"Who wrote this play? My words are mine you must
agree, so why this tangle, mangle and jangle? Trust*

*"Lion's plight, licking limpid leonine lines
to light! Click we must, or face fruitless fines."*

"Fines! I'll find you fine in a nest of snails,
in buckets puffed full with puppy-dog tails!"

*"A puppy dog's right—the role for you. I'd roar
one roar or four to rouse your tired Tiger to soar!"*

"Stop, Sir Lion! Flaccid fights are rarely right,
so I suggest a daring jest for our guests tonight!

"You roar? I'll score! You paw? I'll snore. You gnaw?
I'll claw. You jaw? I'll bore. Take four? Draw more!"

*"Fact is, nothing you can diddle, dance or say
will make me chance another prance today!"*

"So, goodbye, Lion! So long, play! I believe
you'll play Snug, the slug or snail, this eve.

"And, by your leave,
when you crawl upon the floor,
and wail on your sleeve,
suck lemons for an encore,
fall flat on your tail—how I'll grieve!
How I'll snicker seven score,
scorching my paunchy paws sore!"

[Co-author Professor Dee C. Konrad is Associate Judge of the
Tom Howard Contest]

ACCESS DENIED

by **John Howard Reid**

Here I am on View Point Drive
Holiday houses cluster two-a-penny
on this rich man's gambol where private
wharves in winsome white and sleek lakeside
views combine the furled yachts of an ocean-honing
elite with the engine chugging whine of tawdry, time-torn
fishing smacks netting the lake-bed for the seasoned
professional processors on the co-op side of
the bridge. The scent of dollars is over-
powered and undone.

No gap, no track, no inlet
can I find to reach the water's
edge. Each inch is overscored and
underlined, *Private Property. Keep Off!*

But secure, self-serving instincts of a camera
hound overwrite the puny stratagems of caste and
class. No coiled concrete compound, though zebra-barred
or horn-spiked can compete with sudden financial ruin for *This
very night I shall demand thy soul of thee!* Yes, after he'd
junked and demolished holiday home-away cottage
to build a castaway's castle, he'd left his heirs
a benighted inheritance of scruffy, sandy
dunes, transfixed by hopeful weeds!

Staring blindly at swarms of affluent neighbors, loomed a mail-
box, crammed with screeds of advertising creeds and no-blows,
no-loss, no-money-to-pay-till-ransom-day catalogs, hand bills,
dodgers, junk mail.

Why fill a disconnected letter-box servicing yards of prosperous
weeds
and a triple flight of concrete steps to a wharf of half-nelsoned
pylons?

Not one to look a gift access in the mouth, I clambered down
through
a waist-high jungle of juniper, dandelions and seed-tossed
creepers
until my shoes sank into the speckled sand of the bay. Gleaming
gloating neighboring mansions frowned unforgivingly at my
intrusion. Ignoring their disdainful stares, I unstrapped a
camera and with a practised air of cultivated disdain
I clicked all bird-song views at the water's edge.

Shutting the shutter, I took my fill of the sea-
air: The stench of money lachrymose and
seedless; the squalid aroma of sewage
and sea-weed; the sweet perfume
of pinioned fish in the co-ops
across the blaze of haze-
strewn bays. An awe
a worship, a genuine
genuflection. Money
money. All is money
and reading a no-ran
Art is classless crass
Music no more than
mundane echoes of
trash.

How refreshing to
escape the views of
View Point Drive, to
walk on blithely past a
pillaried signpost. Color
bled: *NO LAKE ACCESS*.

MALALAM

by **John Howard Reid**

Pronounced to rhyme with "alarm-'em",
Malalam settles snugly—a strand of weekend
fishermen's shacks—in a brackish backwater bend
of the Silent River. Not marked, even on the largest
map,
Malalam is no more than a spectral cove in the mind,
a mirage
in the days and nights of those who have accidentally
penetrated its
secret.

No roads lead to Malalam, no by-ways or
goat tracks. No access at all, except perched
on the back of the Silent River herself in power-
boat or canoe. No roads in Malalam either, though
the forty-one strung-out cabins are roughly connected
by wayward, winding trails through the close-knit
forest
butting the river's edge.

Natives shun Malalam. "A wizard's lair," they claim.
"A sea-serpent who sleeps by night, by months of
days,
but then awakes to work his sudden sunswept spell
on the
Silent River. One morning, when he has drunk the
dew from

every blade of grass, and all the birds have taken
flight in fright,
every insect winged away, and dormant frogs have
wedged them-
selves into the deepest cracks and crannies of their
tadpoled shoals,
and craven crabs burrowed beneath the shored shards
of sand, he will
appear, uninvited, unwitnessed, unheralded, and
alone."

No sign of his necromantic presence, no lonely
footsteps leading nowhere
on the shore, no surreptitious signs in the sky, just an
ordinary, bright, sunlit
day when the air seems unnaturally still and you can
hear every beat of breath
in your heart. Unknowingly, carelessly carefree, you
stroll unmindfully to that
river's edge and there before your eyes you behold
yourself, crystal clear, in a
world that exactly mirrors that in which you stand.

But which is which? What
is the real world? What is a mere mirror of the real?
Impossible to tell for both
are exact in every detail. No ripples, wave, nor the
slightest edge of movement
betrays the presence of Death. You wait. You try to
stare him down until tides
or time or some stray spark of living life forces him
to reveal which is the real
world, which the mirage.

You stand transfixed. Not daring to move, you stand
staring at yourself in this

identical but alien world. Until the sun finally sets
you free and you force yourself
to rush back to your cabin and nurse your mind
through the nightmares of night, until
dawn allows a brief escape. You will never visit
Malalam again. Except in darker dreams.

MAGIC

by **John Howard Reid**

There are moonbeams where the nectar gathers
from poets private and those in public view;
where storms of silence co-relate with
soulful spirits; energized embers
spark to sudden light; and tiers
of hopeless dreams hustle
away into endless night.

Hidden rainbows lie in
even the severest sun
sceptered sky; snowy
filigrees of star-silvery
oases where flaxeyed
hawks huddle in twos
and threes, dispelling
doubts, forecasting a
universe where souls
are freed from chains
by poets like you and
me.

What is Poetry?

Some guidelines for entering the Tom Howard Poetry Contest

I enjoy judging poetry. It's a snack compared to reading other forms of literature. A story may start poorly, but soon develop into a fascinating character study, a fanciful adventure, an engrossing slice-of-life, or even a riotous comedy. But poetry, you need to read only a stanza or two and you know instantly whether it's going to make the grade to WORTH FURTHER READING or pop instantly into the REJECT basket.

We critics can argue from now to Doomsday as to what exactly poetry is. But we all agree on what it is not. I believe poetry can be and should be anything and everything: A vehicle for ideas, a simple description, an emotion, a thought, a time capsule, a conversation, a tirade and even a story or straight narrative. *The moon was a ghostly galleon, tossed upon cloudy seas; the road was a ribbon of moonlight across the dusty moor; and the highwayman came riding, riding, up to the old inn door.* I don't care that narrative poems are now out of style. If Alfred Noyes can do it, so can you.

I have only one bugaboo. Only one. I will not tolerate doggerel. All other forms, types, genres of verse are welcome. But I don't consider doggerel "poetry". It's just plain simple rubbish.

So what exactly is doggerel? My dictionary says "bad verse." So what makes it bad? In a word: clichés. In doggerel, June always rhymes with moon, never with bassoon or octoroon. Doggerel forms a compulsory ingredient of greeting cards. *A warm hello, a friendly smile, a word of cheer, and then...A special wish that you will soon be feeling well again!* By the humble standards of doggerel, that's actually not too excruciating, but it's still an inevitable candidate for the recycle bin.

Would you believe that 95% of my instant rejects belong to the doggerel class of poetry entries? 95%! I blame the internet's multitudinous non-discriminatory web sites for this sudden rise in the popularity of instant trash. I want no part of it. Yet budding poets will insist on entering this garbage by the truckload. A complete waste of money. There's no way I'd award *A warm hello* a single cent, let alone a thousand dollars.

The worst offenders are religious poets. *I pray to Jesus night and day. He listens hard to what I say.* I'm sure he does! But I'm also sure he's none too thrilled by this insensitive poet's lack of care and creativity.

Next in line are the romantic poets. The moon in June brigade. Running a close third are the philosophers. *The world would be a better place, I think it would be too, if only all the human race, would to themselves be true!*

If you must use rhyming verse, for God's sake, be original!

The poems in this Anthology are a varied lot. But they all have one quality in common: Originality!

Originality!

Originality!

Originality!

Made in the USA
Las Vegas, NV
28 December 2020